the little book of
TAROT

Published by OH!
20 Mortimer Street
London W1T 3JW

Disclaimer:

This book and the information contained herein are for general educational and entertainment use only. The contents are not claimed to be exhaustive, and the book is sold on the understanding that neither the publishers nor the author are thereby engaged in rendering any kind of professional services. Users are encouraged to confirm the information contained herein with other sources and review the information carefully with their appropriate, qualified service providers. Neither the publishers nor the author shall have any responsibility to any person or entity regarding any loss or damage whatsoever, direct or indirect, consequential, special or exemplary, caused or alleged to be caused, by the use or misuse of information contained in this book.

ISBN 978-1-91161-070-0

Editorial consultant: Sasha Fenton
Editorial: Katalin Patnaik, Victoria Godden
Project managers: Jan Budkowski, Russell Porter
Design: Ben Ruocco
Production: Rachel Burgess

A CIP catalogue record for this book is available from the British Library

Printed in China

10 9 8 7 6 5 4

Illustrations: Fer Gregory and bsdgraphic/Shutterstock, piixypeach/Freepik

the little book of

TAROT

katalin patnaik

CONTENTS

INTRODUCTION

Tarot reading took off during the New Age of the 1970s, and it has become immensely popular since then. There are many different decks on the market and many different approaches to reading the cards, but most people agree on the basics, and this straight-forward little book will give you the information you need to make a start as a successful tarot card reader. Many nonsensical myths circulate around the tarot, and here are three:

• You have to be a virgin to read properly
• Only a certain ethnic group may read the cards
• You have to steal your first deck

The real facts are here:

- There are no rules set in stone, only common sense
- There is no governing body or almighty authority that can tell tarot readers how to go about their business
- You don't have to be of any particular parentage to be allowed to read the tarot
- Your ancestors, your beliefs, your skin colour, your gender and your sexual orientation have nothing to do with reading the tarot
- You don't have to be psychic or gifted in any way, either. Channelling spirits might help your readings, but it might confuse the messages too
- What definitely helps, is study – lots of it
- Psychics and mediums also need to study
- You don't need to be given your first tarot deck – many readers would still be waiting for theirs if that was the case

- Many would give up on tarot if they'd received a pack they didn't like and felt they had to use it
- Please do not steal your first deck, but go ahead and buy one without any hesitation

Keeping your deck safe is important – just as you'd keep your mobile phone safe. It doesn't need to be stored in a silk bag, because the box it came in will do. You don't need to perform complicated rituals on your deck; in fact, you don't need to do anything "witchy" to read the cards, but if you like rituals, there are some to choose from later in this book.

Some say you shouldn't read for yourself, but practising would be very hard if you couldn't. It's true that reading for oneself is tricky, because we aren't objective about our own lives. The trick is to read the cards as you would for someone else, list their meanings and remain impartial.

Tarot cards aren't evil, don't open portals to Hell and they won't possess you. They are merely pieces of cardboard with ink on them. The biggest danger you'll face from your deck is a paper cut. The cards are no more evil than birthday cards, both of which remind us of our mortality and our flaws.

Charging money for readings is fine when you are competent enough to do so, and reading the tarot is no more of a gift than being a lawyer, an architect or a chef. Professional readers spend a huge amount of time, energy and money on learning to read the cards, and just as you wouldn't ask an architect to build your house for free, why would you expect a professional tarot reader to work for nothing?

CHAPTER

1

the
MAJOR
ARCANA

A deck of tarot cards comprise two main sections: the 22 cards of the Major Arcana, and the Minor Arcana, which has 56 cards.

The Minor Arcana can further be divided into four suits; Cups, Pentacles, Wands and Swords, each of which contains ten pips and four Court cards. The Major Arcana deals with life's great lessons, the milestones we touch as we progress on our own "Hero's Journey". In a reading, pay special attention to these cards, because they hint at hidden lessons to be learned.

0. THE FOOL

keywords

new beginning, leap of faith, being young at heart, naivety, foolishness, being cheated, intoxication, delirium, childishness, negligence

The Fool is a wild card – it doesn't really belong to any section of the deck, and that is why it is numbered zero. It represents us, the heroes of our own journeys, invested in and enthusiastic about our lives. It encourages us to follow our hearts – but it also cautions us not to do anything foolish.

In a reading, the Fool means new beginnings that are for the better, such as a new job, a new relationship or maybe a new line of study. It also cautions us that someone might make a fool out of us, or that someone is behaving immaturely.

1. THE MAGICIAN

keywords

activity, willpower, creation,
magic, magnetism, passion, a cheater,
a womanizer

The first step on our Journey is the Magician. It shows the stage of exploring the world with full confidence in ourselves and our capabilities. The Magician talks of a strong ego, such as when we are children and when everything revolves around us, but also a strong desire to create and to be active.

In a reading, the Magician means creation and activity. He creates his own reality, and he is not ready to follow others. He is full of energy and enthusiasm, he knows what he wants and he will get it. But be careful, because when his goal is achieved, the Magician is prone to lose interest.

THE HIGH PRIESTESS

2. THE HIGH PRIESTESS

keywords

passivity, knowledge, studies,
spirituality, occultism, intuition,
mysteries, lies, affairs

This card shows how teachers and family members show us how the world works, and this knowledge includes but is not limited to traditions and spirituality. For a toddler, everything is a mystery, and grown-ups are omniscient creatures they can turn to for information. This is a person's first introduction to their world and their society.

In a reading, the High Priestess means mysteries and study of the occult. It urges us to trust our inner voice, our intuition and gut feelings, because they are more accurate than we think. The Priestess can sometimes hint at something that is hidden, such as a lie, a cover-up or an affair.

THE EMPRESS

3. THE EMPRESS

keywords

nurturing, mother, wife, support,
counsellor, therapist, femininity, fertility,
sex, influence, encouragement

The Empress represents the influence
our mothers and matriarchs have on us,
so the way they treat us when we are
completely dependent on them will have
a large impact on how we will treat others
and ourselves later. This stage of life
should mean warmth, safety and security
in our mother's arms.

In a reading, the Empress often shows
a grown-up person – usually a woman.
She has everything she needs for success,
such as wit, knowledge, resources and
support. It is a great card for family
planning or when starting a new business.

THE EMPEROR

4. THE EMPEROR

keywords

control, leadership, father, husband, role model, masculinity, stability, discipline, body builder, dictator

The Emperor represents our fathers, leaders and role models who have shaped our discipline and behaviour. How our patriarchs treat those weaker than them will be a deciding factor in our own stance to leadership, masculinity and emotions. It shapes our view on gender roles and how we treat those less fortunate than us.

In a reading, the Emperor means a grown-up person – usually a man – who does what is expected of him. He knows his duties and he can be depended on to carry them out, but he might not be excellent at showing his emotions, especially tender ones.

THE HIEROPHANT

5. THE HIEROPHANT

keywords

priest, spiritual leader, marriage,
long-term relationship, honesty, faith,
conformity, god(s)

24

We have arrived at the milestone of social conditioning. Culture, traditions and religion leave a heavy mark on us. They keep us out of trouble, but at the same time confine us into the expectations of being "normal". Worrying about "What will others say?" has killed more dreams than lack of opportunities.

In a reading, the Hierophant means a priest or a spiritual leader of any kind. It shows serious intents, loyalty, the possibility of a long-lasting relationship or employment, and a potential marriage. It shows priestly virtues like honesty, caring, being discreet, and having strong faith.

6. THE LOVERS

keywords
love, romance, decisions, choices,
higher self

This card represents our most important and hardest choices in life – and not just in love. Choosing friends, a life partner, our line of study and career all are extremely important decisions that can change our lives forever. If we listen to our heart, or rather to our higher self, we are bound to make the right choice.

In a reading, the Lovers card has two meanings. As the name suggests, one is a romantic relationship that feels like it could be The One. The other is choices and making difficult decisions. In either case, this card is a great omen, showing that we are on the right path.

7. THE CHARIOT

keywords

focus, concentration, control,
goal-oriented, travel, cars,
competitiveness, racing

We need to harness our willpower in order to achieve what we want, and we need to concentrate and to focus on our goals without getting distracted. The Chariot represents perfect control over our minds, and a go-getting attitude that is essential for success.

In a reading, the Chariot shows the need to focus on the situation at hand. We might be hesitating or wasting time or fiddling around rather than going all out for what we want. It also means travel, especially by car. Things will move fast once we make the first steps.

8. STRENGTH

keywords

fortitude, inner strength, stature,
perseverance, brains, tact, logic,
reality check

There are hard times in everyone's life, such as working for a tough exam, or being in a demanding job or a difficult relationship, and we all go through these things from time to time. Strength represents our inner strength and integrity in the way we deal with adversity. This is the lesson many people fail to cope with, because this card shows that we need to use tact, compromises and perseverance rather than weapons and muscles.

In a reading, Strength advises us to use our brain instead of brawn. The situation needs perseverance, calmness and tact rather than brute force. Stay true to yourself and trust yourself. The situation looks worse than it actually is.

THE HERMIT

9. THE HERMIT

keywords

withdrawing, re-evaluation, teacher,
studies, courses, sabbatical leave

The Hermit shows that we need to look deeply within ourselves to decide what is really important and how we can progress further. Finding our purpose and meaning is what needs to happen if we are to find inner peace and contentment. This is the opportunity to get off the roundabout and start working on ourselves.

In a reading, the Hermit advises us to withdraw from the world for a while, to re-evaluate our life and find our purpose. It also means learning and finding a teacher to study further: be it for a hobby or for our line of work, because studying will have the desired outcome.

WHEEL OF FORTUNE

10. THE WHEEL OF FORTUNE

keywords

change, karma, lessons, fate

Avoiding life's roller coaster is impossible, and that is what this card is all about. It shows karmic lessons that need to be learned and cannot be avoided. Whether we are at the top or at the bottom right now, it advises us to remain humble, because the Wheel will turn again.

In a reading, the Wheel of Fortune means a change of our luck, which could be for better or for worse. It reminds us that change is the only thing that is constant, that we shouldn't resist it, though we can control the way that we deal with it. Take control of your reactions and trust in Fate to give you the lessons that you need.

11. JUSTICE

keywords

balance, judgement, truth,
a court case, rules, morality,
ethics, righteousness

Justice represents the moments in life when our morals and ethics are being tested. It could be as minute as returning something small to its owner, or something much bigger, like dragging a criminal to justice. We need to make sure our conscience is clear and that it is aligned with our higher self to be successful.

In a reading, Justice represents moral decisions, the rule of law and, of course, the judicial system. It reassures us that the outcome of our situation will favour the righteous, but it also cautions us to have a good look into ourselves and to be sure that our motives are pure.

THE HANGED MAN

12. THE HANGED MAN

keywords

sacrifice, time out, changed perspectives,
being used, trials, midlife crisis

There comes a moment in life when, after settling down and doing all the introspection the previous cards tell us to do, we still feel stuck. We need to tread the path we have chosen, but we still can't be certain that we are doing what we are meant to. We need to change how we look at things, count our duties and our blessings, and change our mindset.

In a reading, the Hanged Man warns us about people using us for their purposes. We might not receive our dues, or we are readily sacrificing ourselves for the happiness or success of others. The situation needs to be looked at from a different point of view.

13. DEATH

keywords

death, grief, letting go, ending,
transformation

It is time to say goodbye, but the Death card teaches us to let go of something that is important to us, be it a person, a thing or a situation. It isn't easy, but we need to remember that nothing is permanent. The lesson of releasing is one of the hardest, so give yourself ample time to grieve.

In a reading, Death doesn't necessarily mean the physical death of a living thing, because often it is the death of a situation that has been unhealthy for some time. This could signal the end of a struggling marriage, or resigning from a job that you hate. It might mean difficulties in the near future, but this ending is inevitable.

14. TEMPERANCE

keywords

balance, patience, divinity, doctor,
nurse, pharmacist, barista

Finding balance and wisdom is an important lesson that we learn in our lives – and throughout many lives. This is the lesson of finding the divine within ourselves and learning to live according to our higher self's mission. The knowledge that we and the Divine are one blesses us with the state of Temperance.

In a reading, Temperance means taking things step by step, patiently, no matter how enthusiastic and eager we are. We should test the waters first, but we are able to enjoy protection from above, so sooner or later, we might receive a sign that shows us which path to take. It also has some connection with healthcare workers and people working with mixing liquids, such as pharmacists, hairdressers, cooks and baristas.

THE DEVIL

15. THE DEVIL

keywords

bad habits, addictions, abuse,
fear, manipulation, false body image,
bullying, ego

Bad habits, negative personality traits and addictions – everyone has them, although we like to deny it. The beauty of this card's lesson is in its simplicity, so we have to be honest with ourselves and listen to our inner voices. Healthy self-criticism is a key milestone on the way to enlightenment, and this is the time to do a spiritual spring cleaning.

In a reading, the Devil means bad habits and addictions, as well as someone's malevolent intentions towards us. It warns us of dangers from outside.

XVI

THE TOWER

16. THE TOWER

keywords

catastrophe, divorce, accident,
rape, burglary, damage, hurt ego,
escaping turmoil

The Tower means sudden upheavals, and catastrophes that turn our lives upside down. It might feel unbearable at the moment, but when things settle down, there will be a chance for building up a happier, more stable life. Our ego might be destroyed, but we know our place in the cosmic order and we are ready to receive divine knowledge.

In a reading, the Tower means a sudden break, a shock that we did not anticipate and that has destroyed our comfortable everyday routine. It might happen to us or we might cause it deliberately – it will be life-changing nonetheless. It brings the opportunity of a new and better existence.

XVII

THE STAR

17. THE STAR

keywords

wishes, dreams, fulfilment, courage,
exposure, confidence, intimacy,
belief, mission

The Star is one of the purest stops on the Fool's Journey. It is symbolic of the state of mind that happens when we have no desire to prove ourselves to anyone. We know our worth, we know our place, and we do what we came here to do. We trust ourselves and we are aligned with our mission.

In a reading, the Star means a wish that we have worked for coming true, our dreams being fulfilled. It says we are ready to show ourselves to the world, without fears or expectations. It shows a harmonious relationship (with our own body or with a partner) without any secrets or false modesty.

18. THE MOON

keywords

illusions, secrets, backstabbers, femininity, intuition, mediumship, spirit world

It is time to face our "shadow side", our deepest fears and the desires of which we have always been ashamed until now. We might need the help of a professional therapist, but by bringing our hidden side into the open, we become prepared for self-acceptance and eventually for healing.

In a reading, the Moon means that what we see is not the complete truth. There are hidden elements, and maybe even the whole situation with which we are presented is an illusion. It warns us of enemies from places we'd not expect. The Moon also means femininity, intuition and mediumship, so listen to your gut and develop your intuitive gifts.

THE SUN

19. THE SUN

keywords

clarity, love, health, vitality, happiness, enlightenment, success, protection, blessing, childbirth

The Sun means we are ready to enjoy our new life without unnecessary attachments. We have realized that everything exists for our growth, that nothing in this physical world is permanent, and we are ready to find joy in the strangeness of life. It is a blessed state where we can shine our Light on the darkness around us.

In a reading, if there ever was a card that meant "yes", it's the Sun! Whatever you are about to do, this card is a great omen for success, happiness, blessings and protection for you and your endeavours. It has some connection with children, and it brings good news there as well.

20. JUDGEMENT

keywords

reckoning, awakening, forgiveness, growth, being called upon to do something important, moving house

This card suggests that this is a time to make a reckoning: What demons are we carrying with us? What decisions can't we forgive ourselves for? This card teaches us to embrace our demons and to accept them as being parts of human life, and to forgive ourselves for being weak and silly at times. Salvation comes from within. Know that all your decisions have been right for your karmic growth.

In a reading, Judgement means resurrection and hearing the inner call. It is a great sign for budding projects or for court cases. We might face crossroads where both of the options with which we are faced are life-changing. We need to use both intellect and intuition to make this choice. It can also mean moving, especially moving house.

THE WORLD

21. THE WORLD

keywords

success, fulfilment, end of a cycle,
conclusion, closure

The World is the last card of the Major
Arcana and the last stage of the Fool's
Journey before the Wheel turns again
and starts over. It means wholeness and
fulfilment and it says that we have graduated
with flying colours. We have achieved what
we could so far, and we are now celebrating
our success, with the blessing of Spirit.

In a reading, the World means we are
using our skills successfully and we are
in a position to give something back to
society. It advises us to spend quality time
on ourselves and our loved ones. It is a
great omen for anything we have in mind
to do, because it indicates the potential for
fulfilment and success.

CHAPTER

2

the SUIT of CUPS

(also called the suit of Chalices)

Cups represent the range
of emotions we experience
throughout our lives, as
well as our dreams and
even our psychic abilities.

The suit of Cups is associated with the element of Water, and so feelings, devotion and the flow of all kinds of energies are shown on the cards.

Cups can also represent literal cups, as in a cup of tea, a beaker of juice, a pint of beer or a cocktail – and so the tarot Cups are associated with social activities as well.

THE ACE OF CUPS

keywords

love, happiness, intimacy, blessing, harmony, a new start, calmness, clarity

The Ace of Cups represents feelings in their purest form. There is no place for any kind of deception here. It is an especially good sign in love readings, but brings good news in any creative project. Whatever the questioner wants to achieve will need effort, but the situation has the potential for success.

THE TWO OF CUPS

keywords

love, friendship, cooperation, mutual
sympathy, balance, equality, good
relations, forgiveness, reconciliation

This denotes great cooperation, be it in
friendship, family or romantic relationships,
or even a business partnership. There is a
mutual sense of sympathy, equality and caring
that makes everything go smoothly. It shows
something that could last if both parties put
in some effort.

THE THREE OF CUPS

keywords

happiness, fun, girls, or boys, night out, socialising, celebrations, collaboration, friendship, love triangle, jealousy

The Three of Cups is all about fun. Going out with friends for a drink, doing activities with someone with whom you have mutual interests, or big family gatherings straight out of Christmas movies where everyone gets along. But be careful, because there maybe problems under the happy surface.

THE FOUR OF CUPS

keywords

contemplation, re-evaluation, setting boundaries, apathy, saying no, being fed up, burnout

This card means being fed up with the world and just wanting to be left alone. We might feel the need to contemplate our situation and re-evaluate how we lead our lives. Know that you can say no without having to feel guilty.

THE FIVE OF CUPS

keywords

loss, grief, pain, healing from catastrophe, pessimism, realism

This card suggests grief, regrets, sadness and depression, even denial. It could mean losing a loved one (not necessarily to death), a crushed dream, a failed project or even a financial loss. Whatever it is, it will be the only thing we can concentrate on for a while.

THE SIX OF CUPS

keywords

kindness, innocence, pure intentions, friendliness, helpfulness, reliability, nostalgia, curiosity, playfulness

This is the card of kindness, innocence and nostalgia. Small gestures of kindness and help can mean the world to someone in need. It also means pure intentions of friendship, honesty and reliability in a person.

THE SEVEN OF CUPS

keywords

visions, choices, dreams, daydreaming, productive chaos, relaxing order

The Seven of Cups means daydreaming, visions, that we have a choice of many options, even that of creating chaos. This card cautions about the importance of balance. Daydreaming is great, that's how brilliant ideas are born, but if we dilly-dally all day, those ideas will never become reality. It also shows visions from Heaven Above.

THE EIGHT OF CUPS

keywords

self-discovery, cutting ties, abandoning hopeless situations, weariness

This card shows up when it is time to cut the ties. Things were great while they lasted, but now it is time to say goodbye and move on. We have learned what we could, experienced what we had to and a short period of pain is better than long-term depression.

THE NINE OF CUPS

keywords

wealth, abundance, satisfaction, gratitude, pleasure, joy, happiness, indulgence, respect, contentment

This is the card of achievement, satisfaction and enjoyment. This is the time to eat good food, get your hair done, plan a weekend at a spa or pamper yourself. Be grateful for what you have and stay humble, because the Nine of Cups shows humility and niceness in a successful person.

THE TEN
OF CUPS

keywords

happiness, joy, togetherness, family, peace, forgiveness, harmony, counting one's blessings

This is the card of happiness in the near future. No one is eternally happy, but it helps to notice the little snippets of everyday joy and keep them within our hearts for times when the going gets tough. We will soon have a good circle of people around us.

THE PAGE
OF CUPS

keywords

studious, child, youth, open-minded, supportive, clear intentions

As a person, this card relates to a child or someone who is hungry for knowledge. They are nice, kind, supportive and open-minded people whom you can trust with your feelings.

In a reading, it is a good omen for a budding friendship or romance.

THE KNIGHT
OF CUPS

keywords

charming, passionate, adventurous,
new opportunity, womanizer

As a person, the Knight would be a young
adult who is charming, passionate and has
grandiose plans. He will sweep you off your
feet with his personality, but don't expect
anything long-term.

In a reading, it Knight of Cups denotes
an offer that is too good to be true. Look
behind the scenes.

THE QUEEN OF CUPS

keywords

artistic, loving, mediumship, visions, integrity

As a person, this Queen could be someone artistic and loving, who lives life the way they think best. It also means someone with extra-sensory perception and spiritual gifts.

In a reading, the card indicates it is time to be honest with yourself and with others, and to show your true self. You are beautiful just the way you are.

THE KING
OF CUPS

keywords

spiritual, loving, intuitive, inconsistent,
moody, dreams, ideas

As a person, the King is likely to be someone
highly spiritual and loving. He listens to his
intuition and his feelings, but he can be
inconsistent and moody.

In a reading, this card foretells a great idea
that could lead to a successful project, if you
put in the effort and act on it.

CHAPTER

3

the SUIT of PENTACLES

(also called the suit of Coins)

This suit represents life's tangible side, which includes topics such as money, health, family and sensuality.

The suit of Pentacles is associated with the element of Earth, and means stability, support, planting and nurturing, as well as settling down and starting a family. It is also associated with magic, especially with the more down-to-earth kinds, such as herbalism, working with crystals, kitchen witchery and sex magic.

With the suit of Pentacles, things might move slowly but reliably, as long as one is determined enough to achieve one's goals.

THE ACE OF PENTACLES

keywords

new opportunities, money, stability, abundance, family planning, pregnancy, contraception, medication

The Ace of Pentacles means the start of something new that will bring happiness and growth. It's a great card to have whenever there are financial questions to answer. It shows money coming in, abundance and stability. It could also mean family planning, such as taking or coming off contraception.

THE TWO OF PENTACLES

keywords

balancing, juggling, weighing up things, spending less, saving money

This card indicates life's ups and downs. Sometimes we need to juggle our finances at the end of the month, or perhaps we are trying to balance our private life and our work. Try to find the golden middle path in whatever you do, and try to manage your resources more successfully.

THE THREE OF PENTACLES

keywords

teamwork, collaboration, expert advice, skilled labour, confessions

The Three of Pentacles means smooth teamwork and collaboration at work or other projects. It cautions us to ask an expert about the thing we want to do, because we lack proper knowledge – be it legal advice or something practical like the plumbing. It also connects to the church, and so to making confessions.

THE FOUR OF PENTACLES

keywords

greed, hoarding, unwillingness to share, not spending resources, blocked emotions, reserved, bitterness

The Four of Pentacles talks of protecting and collecting something that is important to us, sometimes so much so that we become like a dragon sitting on its treasure – suspicious of everyone, bitter and lonely. Don't lose sight of what is really important.

THE FIVE OF PENTACLES

keywords

loss, troubles, unexpected expense,
poverty, bad health, feeling unloved

This card means serious financial troubles. We
might experience loss, theft or an unexpected
expense. It is a good idea to put money aside
for harder times. Hardships can bring out
the best or the worst in people, so seize this
opportunity to change negative patterns.

THE SIX OF PENTACLES

keywords

fair payment, giving people their dues, charity, fairness, gifts

This card means giving everyone what they deserve. We should aim to pay others their dues without haggling, especially when someone is self-employed. When we have the means, we should help those who are in need. Donating money or time to charities is to be encouraged.

THE SEVEN OF PENTACLES

keywords

coming to fruition, manifestation,
rewards, patience, gardening,
retirement, holiday, leave

This card predicts a time when we have done
all the hard work and are waiting for things to
come to fruition. Our wait will be rewarded
and we will reap what we have sown. It also
shows the time around retirement or taking
some leave.

THE EIGHT OF PENTACLES

keywords

study, apprenticeship, learning, practice, repetition, same old, perfectionism, handicrafts

The Eight of Pentacles means that we are hard at work to perfect a skill. The task might be repetitive and boring, and we need to check if it really takes us forward. If we do it with passion, it is worth the effort. Practice makes perfect.

THE NINE OF PENTACLES

keywords

independence, achievements, success, influence, comfort, time off

This card means standing on our own two feet. We have achieved independence and will not go back to any restricting roles. We can be proud of ourselves and take time to enjoy the finer things in life and spend time on ourselves.

THE TEN OF PENTACLES

keywords

big family, family time, support
system, quality togetherness

The Ten of Pentacles reminds us to spend
quality time with our loved ones and to share
what we have. Group activities are the best
way to bond, like going for a hike, playing
board games, or playing football in the park.
It doesn't take money to enjoy family time, as
we can have fun without incurring expense.

THE PAGE OF PENTACLES

keywords

baby, student, inquisitive, hard-working, stubborn, materialistic

As a person, this page talks of a baby or a young student who has yet to acquire any knowledge. He is inquisitive and hard-working, but he can be stubborn and materialistic.

In a reading, it means an opportunity based on money. It can also talk of a new pregnancy.

THE KNIGHT OF PENTACLES

keywords

patient, dependable, ethical, hard-working, slow-moving, stability, pleasures, promotion

As a person, this card refers to someone patient and dependable, with strong morals. He is determined to achieve his goals, but he won't rush into anything. He strives to achieve stability.

In a reading, it suggests a promotion, stability, long-term relationships, and enjoying sensual pleasures.

THE QUEEN OF PENTACLES

keywords

nurturing, caring, pampering, clever, patient, prosperous, sensual, stable

As a person, this Queen is a motherly figure who nurtures others. She could also be a great business woman: clever, logical, patient and empowering. She knows how to pamper people and she is very sensual.

In a reading, it means a financially stable situation, where you can relax and enjoy the fruits of your labour.

THE KING OF PENTACLES

keywords

practical, courteous, charitable, trustworthy, stability, business, results

As a person, this King indicates a practical, helpful and charitable person who is a true gentleman. He enjoys the finer things in life and likes to share his pleasure with others. He is respected and trusted.

In a reading, it indicates a great business opportunity, stability and the time to see the results of all your hard work.

CHAPTER

4

the
SUIT of
WANDS

(also called Staves or Rods)

This suit talks about
inspiration, action and
movement.

It is associated with the element of Fire, so it represents passion in any form – work, love, offence and defence, hobbies and talents, etc. When we are passionate about something, it is easy to get lost in it; we must be careful not to burn out like a matchstick, but to tend our fire with careful planning and self-discipline. Taking on too many responsibilities will break anyone.

THE ACE OF WANDS

keywords

energy, passion, keenness, willpower, inspiration, creation, sexual interest, 'friends with benefits'

This card represents raw energy, bursting with passion and activity. It shows a person full of inspired energy who will prove themselves to the world. It can also show sexual interest, a passionate lover and in some cases, raw sexual energy.

THE TWO OF WANDS

keywords

plans, goals, taking risks, decisions, discoveries, daring

This card indicates plans and wishes for the future. It is time to think about expanding our territory, and taking steps of discovery into the unknown, before we grow restless and make mistakes. Decide wisely and don't risk everything on an uncertain project.

THE THREE OF WANDS

keywords

opportunities, choices, chances, expanding, further studies, journey through water

The Three of Wands talks of opportunities that lie ahead. You have made the first step, everything's going as expected and you see just how many opportunities and choices you have available. Come out of your comfort zone and let yourself have big dreams, as this will be a time of opportunity for you.

THE FOUR OF WANDS

keywords

stability, reliability, settling down, predictability, strong support, festivities

This suggests achieving stability in life, so you might get the stable, well-paying job with the benefits and perks that you want. It could mean settling down, getting married, or renting or buying your first home. It also shows you are able to rely on a stable family background for support when needed.

THE FIVE
OF WANDS

keywords

quarrels, fights, ego trip, childishness,
showing off, sibling rivalry

This card indicates pointless quarrels,
showing off one's prowess and even taking
part in play fights. This isn't a real argument,
but perhaps a silly, fake one. Sometimes it's
better to step back and agree to disagree.
Don't take things too seriously, but if
something gets out of control, put an end
to it.

THE SIX OF WANDS

keywords

victory, success, conquest, celebration, receiving one's dues

This card denotes a well-deserved victory. You have done what was needed and now you can sit back and receive the praise. Don't let your guard down too long though – continue to work on yourself or you will fall behind.

THE SEVEN OF WANDS

keywords

self-defence, standing up for others, standing your ground, righteous fight

The Seven of Wands means self-defence and being ready to fight for what is right. No matter how hard you try, you can't please everyone, so stand by what you believe and you will have the advantage of being right.

THE EIGHT
OF WANDS

keywords

speed, news, a letter, a message, a
call, post, the internet

This card represents speed! Things will
move fast now and they will go in the right
direction. Imagine that you have thrown a
stone and now want to be where it landed;
that is where you will end up, because your
situation will proceed to where it has to be
– be it good or bad.

THE NINE
OF WANDS

keywords

**weariness, perseverance, defending
beliefs, loyalty**

This card represents a weary warrior.
There have been fights, wounds and
losses; still, you can't give up. You need to
be vigilant, but not at the expense of your
mental and physical health. Ask yourself:
"What am I doing, and is it worth it?"

THE TEN OF WANDS

keywords

overload, overworked, overtired, too many responsibilities, learn to say no, ask for help

The Ten of Wands says you have taken on too many responsibilities. Be it at work, at home or in your community, it is time to start saying no and unloading some of the weight you are carrying. Asking for help isn't a sign of weakness.

THE PAGE OF WANDS

keywords

enthusiasm, playfulness, childishness, carefree attitude, messages, new opportunity

As a person, this Page would be someone young at heart who loves life and is a little childish in that he doesn't take things seriously. He is playful, curious and enthusiastic.

In a reading, this brings a message, good news, a new opportunity, or time to learn something new.

THE KNIGHT OF WANDS

keywords

aggression, plans, energy, enthusiasm, anger, impulsiveness

As a person, this card means that someone hot-headed and impulsive will come into your life. He is full of plans and he starts a lot of projects, but he soon burns out and abandons them.

In a reading, it denotes taking the first step towards one's goal, or a sudden decision that changes everything.

THE QUEEN OF WANDS

keywords

strong, authoritative, leader, bossy, sexy, decisive, headstrong, organizer

As a person, this Queen would be majestic, strong and authoritative. She loves and hates fiercely, and is very good at making decisions.

In a reading, it means the opportunity for a leading role at work or for organizing a big family get-together.

THE KING OF WANDS

keywords

vitality, power, leadership, generosity, passion, focus, sexual prowess

As a person, this card indicates an individual who represents the energy of the sun, possessing vitality, power and generosity. He is a great leader who makes decisions for his subjects' welfare. He is passionate and goal-oriented.

In a reading, it means an opportunity to exercise these qualities.

CHAPTER

5

the
SUIT of
SWORDS

This suit looks scary, but it can be a real ally. It warns us of bad things to come, and prompts us to look for a way to avoid them or to brace ourselves against the storm.

Swords are associated with the element of Air, so they are concerned with communication, intellect and logic, along with mental and physical struggles. In addition, the cards can represent literal swords in the form of scalpels and syringes – and therefore, medical procedures.

THE ACE OF SWORDS

keywords

inspiration, new project, enthusiasm, realization, reality check, communication, injections, operations

This card is a great omen for anything that has to do with logical thinking, writing and communication of any kind. It also shows the need for an honest chat, and a critical look at your situation. It may indicate a visit to the doctor, or medical treatments.

THE TWO OF SWORDS

keywords

defensiveness, doubts, fears, indecision, stalemate, a new perspective

The Two of Swords indicates defensiveness and a fear of moving forward. You might find yourself at a crossroads, unable to decide between two hard choices, bound by doubts and fears. You may need to wait it out, but don't let it turn into a stalemate and stagnation.

THE THREE OF SWORDS

keywords

break-up, divorce, disappointment,
mental health issues, depression,
PTSD, suicidal thoughts,
healing psychology

This is known as the heartbreak card. It suggests
you will not get what you want, or you might get
something but it won't be in the form that you
would prefer. Your plans and hopes will end in
disappointment. It may represent mental health
issues, in which case you must seek specialist help.

THE FOUR OF SWORDS

keywords

rest, regrouping, planning, healing, patience, being alone, mild illness, bed rest

The Four of Swords advises you to take some time out and rest and regroup. It is time to rethink what you want and plan accordingly, which is a typical swords activity. It also advises you to take care of your health.

THE FIVE
OF SWORDS

keywords

cheating, match-fixing, cruelty, malice,
lies, humiliation, failure

This is a card of cheating and deceit. If we already
have our suspicions about someone, it advises
us to be careful with that person and to be safe
rather than sorry. It also suggests that a winner
has been chosen for favours they have done, or
because they have the right connections.

THE SIX OF SWORDS

keywords

moving on, letting go, a journey, a
holiday, moving houses

This card is one of moving on and leaving
the past behind. It is futile to hang on to
something that didn't work out; it's time to
row to new waters and start afresh. It also
means travel, maybe a holiday, a short trip,
or even moving house.

THE SEVEN OF SWORDS

keywords

deceit, sabotage, revenge, disregard
to norms, narcissist, sociopath,
psychopath, rebellion, social uprising

The Seven of Swords indicates sabotage
and openly defying social rules and laws.
This card shows that a person couldn't care
less about other people's feelings.
It often warns us of narcissistic or antisocial
personality disorders. It could also mean
rebellion against oppression or even revenge.

THE EIGHT OF SWORDS

keywords

self-imposed limitations, fear of being different, victim mentality, martyr mentality, surrender

This card represents one's own, unnecessary limitations. Sometimes we believe we are not good enough, that we don't deserve better; we think we have to adjust and make sacrifices if we want acceptance. Thankfully this isn't so, and we just need to gather the courage to set ourselves free.

THE NINE OF SWORDS

keywords

fears, doubts, nightmares, shame, regrets, insomnia, asking for forgiveness, forgiving ourselves

The Nine of Swords tells us about fears and nightmares. Be it actual bad dreams or a rough patch in life, this card warns us not to give the situation more power over us than is needed. Stay true; this too shall pass.

THE TEN OF SWORDS

keywords

defeat, giving up, breaking down,
loss, drama king or queen

This is a card of total defeat. There is no
option left but to face up to failure and
accept it – but how we deal with it is up to
us. It's time to get up, dust ourselves off and
search for the light on the horizon.

THE PAGE
OF SWORDS

keywords

clever, smart, quick-witted, planning
ahead, being prepared

As a person, this Page is clever and quick-
witted. He can get himself out of any
situation, and is mentally ready for anything.

In a reading, it suggests the need to be
careful around such a person, or that we have
to embody his qualities so that we plan ahead
and be prepared.

THE KNIGHT OF SWORDS

keywords

critical, intelligent, rush, brisk, righteousness, social activism, conflicts

As a person, this Knight can be someone who has a sharp mind but who but tends to come to instant conclusions. A brisk personality, he immediately attacks any perceived insult.

In a reading, it foretells a need to protect ourselves or our rights, even if this means fighting for them.

THE QUEEN OF SWORDS

keywords

intelligent, educated, creative, witty, just, pragmatic

As a person, this Queen is highly intelligent and educated. She values intellect more than emotions, and uses hers as a weapon. She is creative, witty and a respected leader. Traditionally this card also represents a widow.

In a reading, this card shows that we must follow the rules. We need to keep a cool head and be pragmatic.

THE KING
OF SWORDS

keywords

talented, organized, rigid, control freak, logic, rule of law, military, lawyer

As a person, this King is very goal-oriented. He can come across as a control freak, because he is highly organized.

In a reading, this card denotes the rule of law. If we want change, we must prepare logical arguments for it.

CHAPTER

6

TOP
READING
TIPS

The prospect of having to learn
78 card meanings can be daunting,
but don't let that put you off.

There is no need for you to sit down
and cram keywords until you know
them by heart, because there are
many easier methods that will make
your learning journey a lot more
enjoyable and, dare I say, fun!
In this chapter you will find tips
and tricks as to how you can make
a personal connection with each
card in your deck, ultimately leading
you to master them all.

A NOTEBOOK

can help you keep track of your
progress, serve as a personal
tarot dictionary, and you can add
information as you go.

PICK A CARD

and list the symbols you see on it. What does that fruit mean? Why does that person make that hand gesture? What is the significance of that colour? Everything is there for a reason – you just have to work out why.

DRAW A CARD

and ask, "What do I need to know about today?" Tarot isn't always life-changing, so if you draw the Death card, it could just mean you'll be dead-tired by the end of the day or you'll watch the last episode of your favourite series on television.

READING
THE CARDS

and asking questions with
this book open will help you
understand the meanings within
the context of the reading.

CREATE SOMETHING

that allows you to meditate over your card's message and to translate it into your chosen art form. The process hardwires the card's meaning into your brain.

LOOK AT A CARD

and memorize every detail, then
close your eyes and imagine
stepping into the scene. What
do you see? What's happening?
What are the characters doing and
what do they tell you? Let your
imagination take control.

CHOOSE A CARD

or a series of cards and tell a
story based on their keywords
or by using the scenes depicted
on them. Does your story have
a happy ending? Which card
would give an unexpected twist
to the tale?

COMPARING CARDS

to each other can teach you to
see connections between them.
Connect cards that have similar
meanings or that are similar in
appearance. Which cards have
directly opposite meanings?

PAIR UP

famous people, celebrities
or even movie or cartoon
characters with your cards
and see how easy it becomes
to remember them! This
works especially well with the
court cards.

JOINING ONLINE GROUPS

can help once you have a basic understanding of your cards. If someone contradicts you, listen to them and take from them only what you find useful. Tarot is a never-ending journey and there's always something new to learn.

Note: Very few people bother with cards that are reversed, so if one turns up the wrong way round, you can either simply turn it the right way or you could consider what it is telling you. It usually means that the situation related to the card is blocked, delayed or weakened.

CHAPTER
7

TAROT
SPREADS

While shuffling, concentrate
on your question,
and when you feel you've
shuffled long enough,
lay out your cards.

Some readers like to lay the cards out face up so the whole picture is visible immediately, while others like to lay them out face down, turn them over and interpret them one by one.

Some spreads have pre-assigned positions for each card, which means each card will have to be interpreted in relation to its position as well as to the main question. You can devise your own spreads, but here are some for you to try.

ONE
CARD

Shuffle the cards, ask your question and pull out one card. This will give you a simple answer to any query. It is a great method to have a quick look, but it will not give you much detail.

PAST, PRESENT and FUTURE

This spread is useful when you want to see the root of a situation and the direction it's heading towards. Shuffle your deck and lay out three cards: one for the Past, one for the Present, and one for the Future. Interpret each card in its position and then look at them together. See the story they tell you.

PAST   PRESENT FUTURE

the
ADVICE spread

Your positions are as follows:

Three cards in a row.

1. Do this
2. The thing you should avoid doing
3. The attitude you need

The first card tells what you are doing right and the second tells you what you could improve or what you might want to avoid doing. The third card will tell you what will be needed for success.

1   2   3

the
HORSESHOE
spread

This is one of the most popular spreads. Start reading at the top left card and work your way around to the last, top right card.

1 Past

2 Present

3 Hidden influences – something that you didn't notice, something under the surface that you aren't conscious of, or something you've been told that isn't true

4 Obstacles – things that are in your way and making it hard for you to succeed

5 Environment – people or circumstances that influence the situation

6 Action that you need to take

7 Outcome

the
CELTIC CROSS

The Celtic Cross is one of the most used spreads of all time and it has countless variations.

Positions

1   The situation
2   Obstacles
3   The root cause
4   The past
5   Goals
6   The future
7   You
8   Your environment
9   Hopes and fears
10 Final outcome

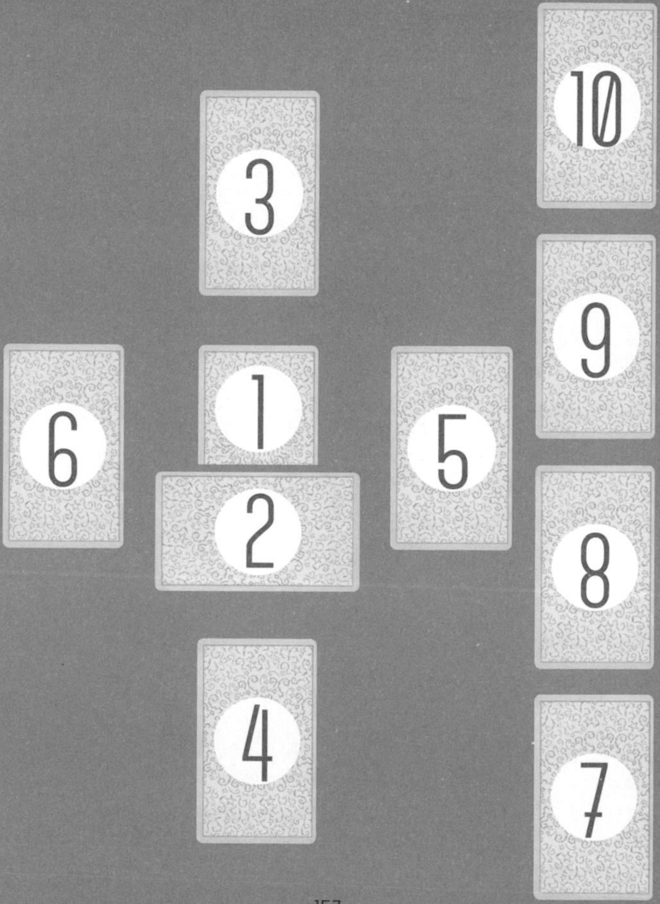
10
3
9
6
1
5
2
8
4
7

CHAPTER

8

TOP TEN TIPS

Spread your cards out in
a long line and ask your
questioner to choose three,
seven or thirteen cards,
just as you like. Now let
the cards lie on the table in
a random layout, and see
what turns up.

- Look out for repeating symbols, such as two Fours or two Knights

- Note the direction in which the characters are looking and how they interact with each other

• See the character's story

• Look out for
connections, so if a King
and a Queen face each
other, the relationship
between the people
they stand for is good,
but if they face in
different directions,
there are problems in
that relationship

• See which suit is dominant

• If you want to know whether something will work or not, see if most of the cards are Cups or Pentacles, in which case, the answer will be positive, but if it is Swords or Wands, the answer will be negative

• Major Arcana cards
will give you a hint as
to the answer

• If the majority of cards are Minor Arcana, the situation is under the seeker's control

• If most of the cards are Major Arcana, the seeker has little control over things and they may be on the receiving end of a karmic lesson

• If there are many Court cards, the situation depends on the cooperation of those involved

CHAPTER

9

USES of
THE TAROT

You can use tarot for prediction, but also for deeper insight into a certain situation, or to check if what you think is really true. But that is only the tip of this huge iceberg. You can use the cards for introspection, vision boards, meditation, magic spells, art projects, inspiration for writing, some forms of psychology and even card games.

You can ask the cards what will happen, how it will happen and when it will happen, but it is worth bearing in mind that what we see is a possible outcome that could change depending on circumstances. You can look into timing, with Wands representing days, Swords as weeks, Cups as months and Pentacles as seasons.

You could ask what needs to happen before your questioners can expect to get what they want – for instance, how to make themselves more attractive to someone they love, so that the lover will propose marriage.

Locating lost objects with the tarot can be fun and very effective. Try it out with something you know the position of. Ask the cards: "Where is my toothbrush?" and you will most likely get cards with water or thrones on them – a reference to your bathroom! Be creative and look at the images rather than the standard tarot meanings.

If you are a medium, you can get confirmation of what Spirit is telling you by following up your channelling with a reading of yourself. In this case, ask for protection and cleanse your deck after each session, by blessing it.

Creating vision boards and using sympathetic or imitative magic can be useful, based on acting out what you want to happen in real life. For example if you want to quit a bad habit, you burn a photocopy of the Devil card, as it relates to addiction.

If you want to be energetic, you can choose the Magician. If you need more patience, you'd choose the Empress.

Many people use the tarot as inspiration, and there are a few books on how to use the tarot for writing. If you need inspiration for art, poetry, story writing, painting or even cooking, ask your cards for advice.

CHAPTER
10

RITUALS

Cleansing, charging, consecrating, essential oils, holy water, incense and candles are not everyone's cup of tea.

While many readers swear you must do or use all these things and more for your cards to work properly, just as many readers roll their eyes at the concept and excel at readings anyway. However, if you decide to use rituals, here are some basics to try out and build on. The act of consecration is a ritual to make your deck more than a bunch of cards, because from now on it will be a sacred tool.

An easy way to cleanse your new deck and welcome it to its new place is by using smoke. White sage, nag champa and sandalwood are all good materials to use, but you don't need to buy fancy incenses or smudge sticks – you can make your own! Bay leaves are great for clearing out unwanted energy, so grab a handful from the kitchen. Open the windows to avoid your smoke detector going off, and also to allow any residual energy from your deck to exit the premises. Light your incense, smudge stick or bunch of bay leaves, and keep it in a fireproof container. Wave your deck above the smoke in one go, or do it card by card, and will the smoke to clear all residual energy.

Hold your deck to your heart and tell it and the Universe that it is now yours, it will only tell you what is true, and it will serve its purpose the best it can.

After cleansing and charging it with your intent, keep the deck on your altar for the night and ask whoever you believe in to give it power and to protect it from negative influences.

Leaving the deck under the light of the sun or a full moon will cleanse and charge your deck, but take care, because strong sunlight might bleach the colours!

Between readings, when you don't have time for complex rituals, a good way to cleanse your deck is to shuffle it and put your intention into it.

You could also blow on the cards to clear any leftover energy. It's the same as shaking your legs after doing exhausting exercise.

Crystals are great for charging your deck, too. Decide what kind of energy you want to give your tarot deck, and keep an appropriate crystal near.

Clear quartz and selenite are excellent cleansers; obsidian and onyx are unbeatable when it comes to protection; amethyst and lapis lazuli are fantastic for intuition; and rose quartz and jasper are great healers.

You can reaffirm the process of blessing and protection before every reading session. Write a spell that feels right to you and that you can use frequently. It doesn't have to be elaborate, but it should state what you expect it to do: give protection, help with interpretation, and assist with expressing the reading in a helpful way.

BLESSINGS
and
SPELLS

Having a prepared blessing and spell is helpful before you start any reading. Try writing your own, but for now here is a simple spell you can use.

Angels, Spirits, Gods
and Guides,

Bless the message my
reading provides

North, South, East
and West,

The Seeker learns
what's for their best.

Light a white candle and imagine a magic circle around you and the table. If working outdoors, you could sprinkle salt in a circle around you, or you could imagine a bright bubble of light surrounding you.

When reading, set firm boundaries regarding the kind of entity that can enter your reading space, and with whom you wish to talk via the cards.

Ask your spirit to tell you who he or she is, and at the end, send the spirit away, undo the magic circle, and then let the candle burn down.

PROTECTION
and blessing from
SPIRIT
GUIDES

Asking for protection and blessing from spirit guides or gods is especially important when channelling spirits with the tarot.

CONCLUSION

Of all the psychic sciences, tarot is probably the easiest to master. Once you get your head around the underlying meanings of each card and learn to put them together to extract their message, you will be up and running. You can use the cards to help you make decisions, to work out whether someone who comes into your life will be right for you, or to see whether the time is right to take some kind of action. Your friends and relatives will be only too glad for you to give them an occasional reading. In time, you may even decide to become a professional reader.